The Zen of Software Development: A Seven Day Journey

A handbook to Enlightened Software Development by Bett Correa

Product of the United States of America

Publisher's Cataloging-in-Publication data
Correa, Bett.
A title of the book : Zen of Software Development: A Seven Day Journey
ISBN-13: 978-1515157366

1. The main category of the book —Computers / Software Development & Engineering / General

First Edition

Editing: Steven Bollhoefer

Dedication and Thanks

This book is for all the people who spend their time planning, designing, engineering, developing, testing, implementing, and maintaining the software which runs our world and helps us live. I hope that it will inspire your teams to work more efficiently and enjoy your time together more.

Contents

Introduction

Do you dream of working on a team of enlightened people who create software which users love? Stop dreaming and start living! This book will get you started on your journey.

Zen is now ready to overtake our offices and enable our teams to create software together. I have laid out exercises you can do alone or with your team members to create a new awareness and Group Mind.

I've spent over 15 years in software development and gone from being a web developer, to a DBA, to a project manager, to a business analyst, to an end to end solutions architect, and a product owner. The pattern I see repeated over and over again is teams missing deadlines, unhappy users, buggy code, and over-budget software. The reasons I blame for this are also the same time and time again: teams fighting, not understanding each other, being stuck in the past, not understanding the users, and overall stressful team environments.

This small handbook lays out a step-by-step process to create a new awareness, first in yourself and then, you'll be surprised to notice, in your team members. I don't waste time on a lot of theory but focus on the facts. The layout is a seven day guide in which you have one small chapter to read each day with an exercise to help give you an awareness of the present. There is also a meditation to practice each day.

The physical exercises should only be done with a doctor's permission! They are meant to be done safely. Listen to your body and only do what you know you can. If you have an injury then don't do something to aggravate it! Use common sense. If you do these exercises slowly and build up you will drastically improve your physical health.

The goal of these exercises is to keep your blood flowing all day. Blood flow allows your brain to function optimally and enables you to be present. If you are nodding off because you are comatose you won't be able to focus.

Sitting all day is very dangerous. Google it. Based on my research I recommend getting up and doing some kind of exercise every ten minutes. The exercise I do at my desk is usually squats. If you can get your teammates involved, try it. If circumstances aren't very positive you can just stretch and march in place for 20 seconds, then five times a day go to an empty conference room to do the other more extensive exercises. The exercises are meant to be done several times a day and take two minutes or less. For instance, I do them three to five times a day in an empty conference room. I do no other working out except for pull ups a few times a week. Spending hours in a gym is a hobby which you can participate in if you so choose, but is not necessary. You can get all the exercise you need in five small two-minute sessions each day. I recommend that after the first week you mix up the exercises and do them in some combination several times a day. You should continue doing them even if you routinely visit the gym.

How to read this book:

Read a chapter a day to begin your seven day journey to a new awareness. There are three parts to each day. One is the write up, the second is the meditation, and the third is the physical exercise. Give yourself time to do the 15 minute meditation. The exercises are cumulative; after the first week you can do several each day. If you miss a day, don't beat yourself up. That only creates drama and stress; just move on and start again the next day. Don't give up either, these methods are time-tested and work. I recommend repeating the meditations each week until you feel the changes you hope you get. Be patient on your journey, enlightenment is a process and you can either reach it in one moment or in ten years.

Read on, and enjoy the life-affirming journey!

Day One - The End State

You might find it strange to start this journey of enlightenment with a chapter on how software could be created, but, "it's best to start with the end in mind," as our friend Steven Covey says. Have you thought about your perfect team environment? How do team members treat each other? How does it feel to get up each morning to head to the office? What are design meetings like? How about planning meetings? How about post-mortems? Go ahead and close your eyes and envision your perfect team environment. Now write down a few of the key quality attributes of your vision. Review your list. Does it include anything like "Does not have..."? Remove those and rewrite them as positive statements, as the mind only understands positive ideas. Make sure you have at least three solid short statements describing your environment, this will be your end state.

Every day you will spend 15 minutes meditating by finding a quiet place where you won't be disturbed. In this quiet place you will focus on breathing. Completely fill your lungs on each inhalation and completely empty your lungs on each exhalation with no breaks in between. Breathe through your nose at a normal pace, not slower or faster. Sit completely still. You will have something to meditate on during your session. On each inward or outward breath say the next word in your mantra, for example:

Inhale: my

Exhale: team

Inhale: listens

You should repeat this for a few minutes, then move to the next statement that you've written.

During your 15 minute daily meditation today, use the statements you've written during your envisioning exercise.

Other notes on the daily meditation:

If you find that your mind wanders, return your focus to your breath. It might take several sessions to train your mind not to wander. You might feel the urge to move around and look at things on your phone. Learn how to sit still and focus on your breath.

You might want to listen to nature noises, Tibetan glass bowls, or other ambient music to help you concentrate.

Put your phone on airplane mode to prevent people from messaging you.

Presence is a real discipline which can be learned. You can do it.

Physical Exercises - Warm up the body

These exercises will warm up your body and you should do them a few times each day. They move blood through you and will enable creativity. If your office is very enlightened your whole team can do them at the beginning of a meeting and even somewhere in the middle if it's a long meeting. I personally sit on an exercise ball so I move around all day, and I feel it really helps keep my mind active.

Wrist rolls

Shoulder rolls

Neck rolls

Hip rolls

Knee rolls

Ankle rolls

Day Two - Resistance is Futile

There was a developer who complained every day about the bad requirements he had to deal with. He would go on and on about his knowledge on how good requirements were written. He spent a lot of energy on this and felt a lot of pride in self-righteously making sure everyone knew that he knew how things Should Be.

The desire for things to be different from how they are is the reason you are reading this book. Good! But we need to realize that actually resisting reality is simply insane. The first step to enlightenment is Radical Acceptance of Reality. This might seem completely counter intuitive to you right now but you will find that as you accept each thing that is “wrong” and “unfair” within your team you will slowly gain a new peace of mind.

When we resist reality we don't solve anything, instead we create suffering and conflict inside ourselves. Ego trips, incomplete requirements, unrealistic project plans, and boring meetings are all a result of resisting reality.

Today you will write a new list comprising all of the things that are terribly wrong with your work. Describe how your boss is unrealistic, how your project manager lacks organizational skills, how your architecture is out of date and is crippling you, your executives are unrealistic, and your users ignorant sots. Good!

Now rewrite the list as follows: I accept < item>.

“Wait!” you are screaming. “This is WRONG! Accepting these terrible things isn’t why I picked up this book!” Until you accept reality you can't start to change it. You must radically accept reality! Your constant resistance against What Is is causing you mental suffering. Each day your suffering grows and you do anything you can to avoid it. You might have picked up drinking coffee, smoking, or drinking alcohol after work just to sedate the suffering that you feel all day at the office. You might go to your favorite website to escape the mental agony of another planning meeting or let your mind drift to another place during a staff meeting. These are all signs that you are trying to escape the present moment. Only by accepting What Is can you engage in the present.

Your daily meditation today is to meditate on each of the items on your list and accept them. You must accept them truly, not just say the words in your mind.

Physical Exercise - The jumping jack

Jump in the air throwing your arms up

Come down and bring your arms down too at your sides

Do a few and as the weeks go on you can add more. As you get better you can do jumping squats.

Day Three - Be the Change

Three developers sat around a break room table. The first developer opened his lunch and said, "Oh yum, beef brisket!" The second did the same and declared, "Wow, delicious red curry." The third developer opened his and said, "A ham sandwich on white bread! Not again, I hate this!" The second day the first two developers opened their lunch and found good things to eat and were happy. The third opened another ham sandwich on white bread, "Why?" he exclaimed. This went on for another week until he finally shouted, "If this happens again I am going to kill myself!" The next day the first two again opened their lunches to find wonderful things to eat. The third opened his and then immediately took his fork and stuck it into his jugular. The first developer said to the second, "Why did his wife do this to him?" The second developer stated, "He packs his own lunch."

The truth is we all pack our own lunch. We get what we get because we act like we act. It's only funny because it's so true. When we walk into a meeting with a strong desire to be right and a fear of looking bad, we end up fighting and arguing over things that we later realize were a waste of time. We have to change ourselves in order for our environments to change. Accepting the reality of what's currently wrong is only the first step, we must also realize the other things we are holding on to, such as resentment and anger about past failures of ourselves and our teammates. These memories stick in our minds and we dwell on them incessantly. We bring them up during meetings and think about them while working on something new. Maybe things were better in the past because the managers used to listen to us and respect us, or we wish things could be simple and efficient like they were before the users adopted a new hardware system that makes everything too complicated.

But it's not just the past that is an issue, we also fear the future issues our software will have. The lead will quit and we'll get stuck with more work, the users won't adopt the software, the funding will run out. These worries don’t have to be negative, they can also be positive hopes which keep our minds occupied. As soon as a new project manager is hired things will get back on track, the new infrastructure being built now will make all changes in the future so much easier, or a new tool that will be bought next year will change everything and life will be good.

Being fixated on the past or on the future is a distraction from the present; now is the only time we can make an impact.

When we focus on thoughts of the past or the future we lose our ability to be aware. Awareness of the present is the most powerful force we wield. When you come to work with a strong presence you will Be the Change.

Today make a list of the things you are focused on from both the past and the future, whether they be positive or negative. Your meditation is to accept each of these and release them. For example, "I accept that the users might not like our new software." or, "I accept that the previous product owner listened to us and the current one doesn't." Acceptance is the first step towards freedom.

Physical Exercise - The dip

Slide to the front of your seat and put your hands on the edge. Then move your butt out from the seat and lower yourself as far as is comfortable.

Lift back up slowly. If your chair has wheels this will add extra difficulty as you keep the chair from rolling!

Do a few at first and slowly add more over the weeks.

Day Four - Fear is the Mind Killer

The only time that action can be taken is now and to do that you have to be aware of the present. Many things can stop you from being present, and one of the most powerful is fear. Fear can strike you while you are sitting in a meeting or at your desk coding and is sparked when you suddenly realize or hear something that causes fear. Your thoughts begin to swirl as your mental functions are taken over by worries about the implications, the dangers, and the potential disaster.

For instance, you might have a fear of losing face in front of your boss. When someone triggers this fear by bringing up a fault in your work you might have a flood of fear flow through your body. Your brain is awash in the stress hormone cortisol. You are in fight or flight mode and this fear stops you from thinking critically and responding correctly. Instead of digging patiently and methodically into the issue at hand you react out of fear. You blame someone else quickly without calmly considering the comment.

When you are in a state of fear or worry it's impossible to live in the present. Fears happen in a moment and can cause you to lose your ability to function which will greatly impact your ability to succeed in each task assigned to you, to work with others, and to get promoted. The buzz word around the ability to control your reactions is Emotional Intelligence (EQ). Those with high EQ are shown to be much more happy and successful in life. If you can learn to recognize the rush of emotion and not react, then you can start developing your EQ.

Write down the things you are afraid of. This will grant you new awareness and allow you to recognize their hold on your mind and to stop fixating on the fear.

You can also learn how to overcome the fear in the moment so that you can continue to function. To stop fixating on a thought, you should become an observer of your own mind. Ask yourself, "What is my next thought?" Become aware of how you think. Write down your common thoughts. You'll realize that your mind has a message it wants you to believe. Your mind isn't your friend. It wants to hold you hostage. You need to become the observer of your mind so you can quiet it.

Accept the fear. Let it wash over you. Feel it, let it go, and then return to the moment. What is really going on? Now your mind is clear and you can focus with a quiet mind on the present. Ask yourself what your teammate is really saying instead of reacting to the fear. This practice takes a lot of effort and you will fail many times before you can start quieting the fear. Even when you fail you must not beat yourself up. Accept yourself as you are. Meditate on, "I am a presence experiencing this feeling."

Physical Exercise - The Squat

Stand up from your chair and take a tiny step forward. Sit down, but don't let your butt touch the seat. Go as low as possible. This position keeps your posture correct.

Stand up slowly. Ensure that your knees never go in front of your feet.

Do as many as you can slowly.

As you get better at this you can add a jump.

Day Five - Love the Pain

We talked about fear, but there is a more specific fear that is the fear of pain that can overtake our minds and even create our identity. We might not even be aware of how much pain we are in everyday because we spend all our energy trying to escape it. I've talked about escapes from the present before, and pain is caused by not accepting our present reality. The only way to really escape pain is by embracing it, whether it is the pain of sitting through another staff meeting, the pain of telling your manager bad news, or the pain of losing out on a promotion.

Software has many areas for potential pain such as analyzing requirements, QA, testing, user training, project management, security evaluations, and so on. There are also the areas around software development including unit testing, writing good code documentation, writing user friendly release notes, working with people in different time zones, releases, outages, and working with difficult people. *Each of these can be transformed into thrilling areas if you can learn to accept and even embrace pain.*

Changing your viewpoint will not only allow you to focus during previously painful tasks but also make you excel at them. If you once avoided doing tool evaluations but now you embrace them, you might be the only one in the office who actively starts seeking out this work. Your team will start looking up to you and respecting your opinions in this area.

Taking a specialty that others find painful and embracing it is one of the best ways to get noticed and succeed. Usually we look for any escape from our pain, and you already have your list of things you do to escape pain, don’t you? Today write a list of the pains you are avoiding. Rewrite it with "I embrace the pain of <item>."

Go through the list and meditate on each one, focusing on really embracing it. You might not be convinced that you can transform the pain into enjoyment, but you can only find out if you truly try. This might be very difficult, which is why this seven day journey is meant to be repeated many times. Each week you can get closer to truly accepting the pain you face each day, and only then will your suffering be eliminated.

Physical Exercise - The Plank

Speaking of pain, it's time to do the Plank. Put your hands on some paper towels. Keep your body in a straight plank with your arms in the top of a push up position.

Hold your body here for as long as you can. You can set a timer.

As you get the duration longer and longer you can practice tightening up your entire body during the whole time. Feel each muscle tighten up. This body awareness will make the exercise work even better. Stay focused during each of the times you do any exercise from now on.

Day Six - The Enemy Within

Have you heard this voice in your head yet? "Wow, you really suck at meditating! You can't stop worrying, and you avoid pain like the plague. This whole Zen of Software Development crap doesn't work for you! Move on and enjoy life!"

If so then you are not alone. When I started meditating I failed so many times. I wanted to give up. I would come up with any excuse! *That's because being present is very hard to experience. It actually hurts.*

We suppress our real feelings and therefore suffer most of the time. Our minds have been programmed to only dwell on the past and on the future, and they treat all events as triggers to move to one of those two extrema. Eventually we spend very little time in the Now. Thus we miss important requirements our users are asking us for and we miss important design impacts because we are fighting over ego issues instead of being focused on the design.

Suffering is often a prelude to enlightened. Viktor Frankl lived in several concentration camps and wrote about them in *Man's Search for Meaning*. He learned much about how man can find meaning despite terrible conditions. If we go along and nothing is terrible in our lives then we might never wake up; we could just live an unfulfilling life and die. But you don't need to have terrible suffering before you wake up and realize that this moment matters. You can do it now. You can make your life full of peace and joy. You have everything you need now, but to realize it you need to think about the end state. Not the one we talked about in Chapter 1, but the one which your physical body will end up in: your death bed.

The answer to getting present is realizing This Moment Matters. We often don't get this realization until we are faced with death. We live our lives as if each moment should be escaped from and we push off action because we are too scared. We don't treat the present as a moment that matters; we act like the here and now is just a drudgery to get through. Visualize yourself on your death bed, what message would your dying self whisper to you with its last breath? Your mediation today is “this moment matters.”

Physical Exercise: The Jumping Lunge

If you feel jumping is too much, start with just a regular lunge.

Place one leg in front of the other. Bend it at a 90-degree angle.

Allow the other leg to stretch out behind you in a straight line.

Drop your body between your two legs slowly. Only go as far as you feel safe. Lift back up slowly.

When you come back up, jump on the front leg. Land softly without losing your balance, then go directly back down into another lunge.

Do a few and start switching legs halfway through. Add more as the weeks go on and you gain strength.

Day Seven - My Body is My Home

At this point you might be wondering what our physical bodies have to do with the clarity of our mind. Each day I recommended a physical exercise and a meditation. Both are critical. Even the Bible calls our bodies our temples. When we are escaping from feelings like pain and fear we often eat, drink, smoke, and ingest things which help us leave the current moment. These substances, whether they are fast food, candy, alcohol, cigarettes, or marijuana, help us sedate our pain and anxiety. We crave them, need them. Otherwise we Feel. Yes, we Feel.

Feelings are strong and overwhelming, and as a child we are taught to suppress them rather act on them. However feelings need to be felt and then they should be let go, not suppressed. Using a substance so we don't feel and not dealing with our feelings in a healthy way will stop us from being present.

Take some time to think about the ways you sedate and control feelings through food, drink, and other substances. Going to the core of your drives to get another <item> will not only help you become a focused person but also realize their negative impacts on your body.

All of this distraction from feeling is killing our bodies and making our minds numb. Accepting our feelings and feeling them deeply will allow us to start making healthy changes.

When we realize that we've been poisoning our bodies for many years we can gain the strength to no longer want to overeat or consume food that harms us. We start recognizing the craving for sugar and salt as escapes. There are lots of studies on how dangerous sugar is for you, and even small amounts can destroy your body.

We can take the first steps to stop trying to escape from pain at this moment and choose instead to accept that pain. As we learn to accept physical pain we can begin to accept our feelings also.

When a strong feeling comes over us, such as anxiety, boredom, fear, or pain, let the feeling wash over you. Feel it deeply. There is no need to try to see what the source of the feeling is. Don't narrate your feeling. The voice in your head will want to talk about the source of the feeling and blame others for it or tell you why it happened and how it will continue. This is no longer feeling the original feeling but instead turning it into drama. Just feel it deeply, let it go, and once it has passed you can keep moving, coding, or focusing on a meeting. You'll find that you didn't even need to get the substance you usually use to try to relax. You'll have naturally relaxed, and over time this practice will change your whole life. Today meditate on, "I feel deeply."

Physical Exercise: The Pushup

Use paper towels and keep your body completely straight. Keep your arms as close to your body as possible for a triceps push up, or hold them out at 90 degree angles for a biceps pushup.

The Beginning of the Journey

Whoa, you may have done what I sometimes do and have skimmed this book quickly to see what it's all about before reading it more carefully. If so, you should know that the results only come from daily exercise and meditation. If you did practice these each day then you will have come a long way and may be wondering where to go from here. I have a list of recommended books below which go much more in depth into these issues than this short handbook, but the best advice I have is to keep meditating. You can re-read this book and use the meditations here or come up with your own. The steps I give are mainly to kick start your journey and give you a taste of the enlightenment that is possible. I've been on this journey for many years and I still have to meditate each day, observe my thoughts carefully, and catch myself when I fall into pain avoidance and cycles of worry and fear.

The key to each day, each hour, and each minute is to be grateful for that moment. Each moment is a gift, and the previous moment is gone. This moment now is the only one where you can do great things.

The First Day's List

Pull up the list you made on day one and feel for a moment what you would feel if all of the positive items were present. These changes are possible and all start with you, but remember not to get caught up in the future. You might now realize that some of the items can be combined.

For example if you had, “project manager is realistic,” and “manager respects us.” You now realize that in your perfect environment both are present and both are listening. In your perfect work environment no one lives in the past/future or spends their time reacting to their fear and pain.

At first your team members might not notice your change, but don’t worry. Keep focused on the present and eventually not only will they notice but they will start changing also. It’s impossible to fight with someone who is totally present. As you continue to repeat the meditations laid out in this book or move on to your own meditations you will find that your team starts becoming more present as well. The energy you bring will inspire them to also be more attentive and focused. Those who can't handle working around someone so engaged might end up quitting or being fired as the manager starts comparing people to you. The team will slowly change, and accepting the present is your key to success.

In some bad cases your new acceptance of reality will show you that your current team will not work with your new present attitude. Your fear might have been keeping you from trying to find a new team. You might have been more afraid of finding a new position than of stagnating in your current job. Once you accept reality and see your fear and pain avoidance clearly you could decide to move on and find a more enlightened company to be a part of.

The Physical

The physical exercises are also just the beginning. With each one you should focus on the muscles that are tightening up during the exercise. Find ways to add things to each exercise to keep it challenging, such as longer duration, more controlled movements, additional repetitions of each exercise, or more workout periods in the day. These exercises are really all you need to have a healthy body, no gym is required! Also make sure you don't sit for more than ten minutes at a time. You'll notice as you do the meditations and these exercises that you'll start wanting to eat more healthily. Try cooking all your own meals on the weekend then you can have a lunch ready to bring and won't be tempted by fast food during the week. Restaurants and processed prepackaged foods use a lot of sugar and unhealthy oils, but as you learn more about cooking you can cook food that tastes good and fuels your body with what it needs.

As you allow yourself to feel, the need to escape by eating unhealthy snacks, drinks, or other substances will disappear and you will find your health improving. Your concentration will be much better when you cut out sugar. Your sleep will be sounder when you cut out caffeine and alcohol. Your digestion will be better when you cut out carbs and unhealthy fats.

The Future

Now more than ever are the techniques laid out in this book needed. Customers demand new product and service features and will quickly move to a new product and service provider for almost any reason. Diverse platforms and security concerns drive ever more complex systems. Remote teams decrease easy face-to-face communication. At the same time, more and more of our lives depend on software. This means those software teams who can overcome these complications with presence will succeed in the competitive software industry. The software professional who can succeed in this environment by using presence will be in high demand.

Your Journey Outside of the Office

All the moments in your life matter both inside and outside of work. I wrote this book with the narrow focus of being used inside of a software development team, but these ideas can and should be applied to every aspect of your life and will give you a new found purpose and desire to grow.

Socially you might develop a larger, deeper network of relationships. As you become more and more present at work you will discover rich relationships with your coworkers. These might spill over into an enriched social life, deeper friendships, and lifelong friends.

Your personal life will change also. If you have a family your spouse and kids will notice your new presence. Instead of texting at dinner or watching TV you might spend more time engaged in meaningful discussions. You might realize that many of your after work activities are mainly used to sedate the pain you accumulate during the day. When you cut those out and start coming home with a refreshed satisfied feeling you will want to be engaged after work also.

Your younger kids will respond with delight. You will find willing participants in them. You might get more involved in their homework, tutoring, sports, arts, and other activities. They will be truly delighted.

If you have teenagers they might find this newly present parent annoying. For them it could be some time before they engage with you. Be patient with your teens. Listen and do what the moment calls for. Use all your techniques to stay focused and present.

For your spouse you might have a lot more difficulty. If you were truly in full pain avoidance mode at work for a long time you probably have lost touch with your spouse. Your spouse might have adapted to your habits and started pain avoidance habits of their own. You have lots and lots of work to do to reconnect, and you might end up finding out that your spouse isn't willing to be present with you. This could end up making your life much more difficult than you may imagine, but the possibility of living as a couple of engaged present people could make the journey worthwhile.

Outside of your family you may start being interested in being present in other things. You could start looking for new hobbies and activities that you can be involved in. You might pick up a cause to support, a musical instrument, or a new physical activity. The possibilities are endless as life is full of intricacies to be explored and enjoyed.

You also might have the reverse. You might realize that you were involved in too many activities that kept you busy and now you want to do less. Cutting out things that don't benefit you is a big step in becoming present. Ask why you are doing the activities that keep you busy.

Use the death bed image of yourself again. Visualize yourself on your death bed and ask yourself what you would regret if you didn't get to experience it. Our lives have many aspects and as we become more present we want to stretch and explore them.

Bett's Story

So far I haven't really shared anything about my personal journey in this book. I've been in software development since 1999 and became a software architect in 2007. I now focus on the customer aspects of software development, doing research and design. My journey began after September 11th, 2001 when I realized that I wasn't going to live forever. This glimpse into my own mortality made me do a death bed visualization exercise and I realized that I love to create.

My first professional step was to move closer and closer to pure creation at work. I realized that listening to users, subject matter experts, and developers gave me such great insights that I could manage to build solid designs just by paying close attention. I also learned to embrace the pain of software requirements. These two skills, listening and embracing the pain, set me up to quickly become an expert on my projects. I gained a reputation in each project with the culmination of being promoted to software architect. You can read my career story in my first book, *You Can be a Software Architect.*

In my personal life I realized that I wanted to write, which is what I did as a child. I started to write lots of very bad short stories about action heroes before eventually realizing that it would be more fun to write about my main passion, software. I've also written several novels and other books over the last 11 years. I picked up public speaking and greatly enjoy sharing my insights in front of a room. I grew from speaking to improv acting and now I have a musical improv group. All of these activities require absolute presence, as if I make a mistake on stage I need to move on and not get caught up in emotions and anger, which is true for all team interaction. I love teaching improv techniques to development teams, which include things as simple as listening to your teammates and making them look like stars. Implementing these ideas can quickly turn a team around.

I also have a podcast where I interview software professionals. I speak at various software conferences each year while continuing to work in the industry to see the challenges that teams are faced with each day.

Recommended Reading

Books I recommend on continuing your journey into enlightenment:

Freedom from the Known by Jiddu Krishnamurti

The Power of Now: A Guide to Spiritual Enlightenment by Eckhart Tolle

The Presence Process: A Healing Journey Into Present Moment Awareness by Michael Brown

Alchemy of the Heart by Michael Brown

To dig into more of philosophy behind enlightenment I also recommend:

Letters from a Stoic by Seneca

Meditations by Marcus Aurelius

Self-Reliance by Ralph Waldo Emerson

The Essays of Montaigne by Michel de Montaigne

Software related books that use these principles:

Scrum: The Art of Doing Twice the Work in Half the Time by Jeff Sutherland

The Phoenix Project: A Novel About IT, DevOps, and Helping Your Business Win by Gene Kim

Additional Physical Exercises

The Pull Up

Burpees

Mountain Climbers

Side Planks

Back Strengthener

About the Author

1

Bett Correa, author of several books, professional public speaker, Distinguished Toastmaster and former Presidents Distinguished Division Governor in Toastmasters and winner of Division Governor of the Year award, has been in IT since 1999, first as a developer then in 2007 she became a Solutions Architect at Verizon. Bett also hosts the Zen of Software Development Podcast. Now, she is a Customer Experience Architect improving the processes and the customer experiences in software design. Her books are available on Amazon and Audible.

Bett has several more books coming out soon. Keep up on the latest of her events, books, articles, speaking engagements.

Listen to her Podcast at: ZenofSoftwareDevelopment.com

Follow her on Twitter @betterworkINC.

Follow her blog at www.betterworkinc.com

Sign up for her newsletter at http://eepurl.com/f_ETX

www.ingramcontent.com/pod-product-compliance
Lightning Source LLC
Chambersburg PA
CBHW070928050326
40689CB00015B/3656

9781515157366